EVERYDAY CAT EXCUSES

Why I can't do what you want

Written & Illustrated by Molly Brandenburg

STERLING

New York / London
www.sterlingpublishing.com

STERLING and the distinctive Sterling logo are registered trademarks of
Sterling Publishing Co., Inc.

Library of Congress Cataloging-in-Publication Data

Brandenburg, Molly.
    Everyday cat excuses : why I can't do what you want /
    written and illustrated by Molly Brandenburg.
      p. cm.
  ISBN-13: 978-1-4027-5903-1
  ISBN-10: 1-4027-5903-7
  1. Cats—Humor. 2. Excuses—Humor. I. Title.

PN6231.C23B73 2008
818'.602—dc22

                     2007050343

2   4   6   8 10 9 7 5 3 1

Published by Sterling Publishing Co., Inc.
387 Park Avenue South, New York, NY 10016
Previously published in paperback as *Everyday Cat Excuses*
by Potatohead Press and © 2006 by Molly Brandenburg
First Sterling edition published in 2008.
Distributed in Canada by Sterling Publishing
^c/o Canadian Manda Group, 165 Dufferin Street
Toronto, Ontario, Canada M6K 3H6
Distributed in the United Kingdom by GMC Distribution Services
Castle Place, 166 High Street, Lewes, East Sussex, England BN7 1XU
Distributed in Australia by Capricorn Link (Australia) Pty. Ltd.
P.O. Box 704, Windsor, NSW 2756, Australia

Sterling ISBN-13: 978-1-4027-5903-1
ISBN-10: 1-4027-5903-7

For information about custom editions, special sales, premium and
corporate purchases, please contact Sterling Special Sales
Department at 800-805-5489 or specialsales@sterlingpublishing.com.

This Book
is Dedicated
to the memory
of Joe Ranft

THIS IS A BOOK ABOUT CATS.

They live with us, among us. They have fur. they gnaw on
fish heads and chase balls of lint. They bring us gifts of
dead, mold-covered mice. They are striped, spotted
or tuxedoed. And yet, they will not do our bidding.

Why? They have excuses. Excuses for when they wake up,
excuses for when they fall asleep in a pile of other cats.
Excuses for every hour of the day. Enough excuses, finally,
to fill up a book. This book. Read it, and learn the truth.
Before they use all their excuses on YOU.

HEY, I'M SORRY I CAN'T DO WHAT YOU WANT TODAY, BUT I'M REALLY BUSY... OKAY?

I CAN'T BECAUSE...

I'M SALIVATING.

I'M SHEDDING.

I'M HAVING KITTENS.

I CAN'T BECAUSE...

I NEED TO GO
OUTSIDE.

I NEED TO GO INSIDE.

I REALLY NEED TO
GO OUTSIDE.

NO, HOLD ON, I
ACTUALLY REALLY
NEED TO GO INSIDE.

OKAY, OKAY, OKAY.
LET'S START OVER.
OKAY, WHAT REALLY
NEEDS TO HAPPEN IS, I
NEED TO GO OUTSIDE.

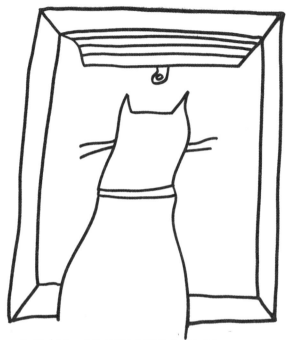

OKAY—JUST LET ME IN—
NOW. I DON'T CARE WHAT
I SAID BEFORE. I WAS CRAZY,
LOCO, NUTS. I HATE OUTSIDE.
I WANT INSIDE. NOW.

NO WAIT, OKAY, ACTUALLY
WHAT I REALLY NEED IS—
OH FORGET IT.

LOOK I'M REALLY SORRY, BUT I CAN'T BECAUSE...

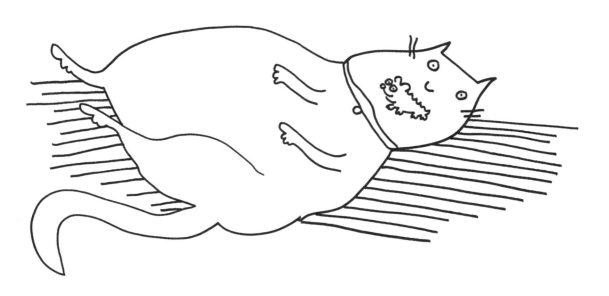

I'M CHEWING ON A SQUEAK TOY.

I'M WORSHIPING
YOU FROM AFAR.

LET ME RUN THIS BY YOU AGAIN. I CAN'T BECAUSE...

I'M GNAWING
ON A DEAD FISH
I FOUND IN A
GARBAGE
CAN.

I'M FLAT.

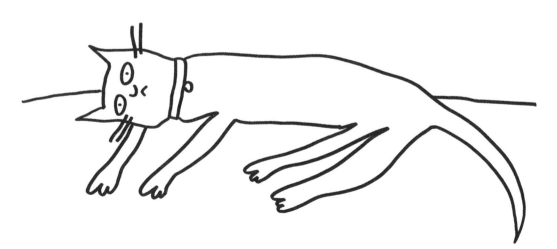

I'M BONDING
WITH
MY FLEAS.

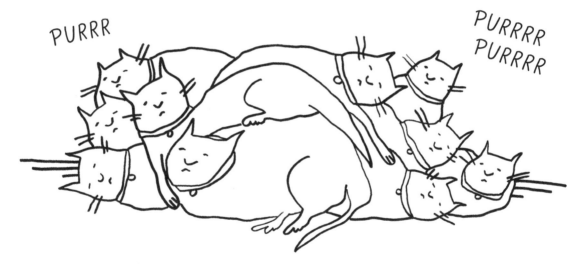

I'M SLEEPING IN A TEN-CAT PILE UP.

LOOK, I AM NOT EVEN
KIDDING, OKAY?!!!

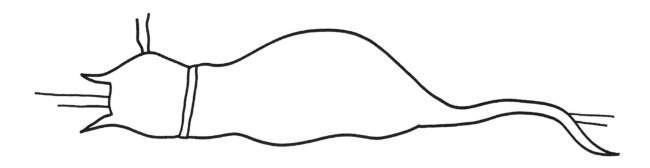

GET LOST, I'M ASLEEP.

Writer/illustrator/animal lover Molly Brandenburg has had her work published in the alternative press as well as national publications and major corporate media. Also a comedy performer, Ms. Brandenburg is known to cabaret audiences for her acclaimed one-woman show, *The Peggy Jude Comeback Tour.* This book was inspired by her weight-challenged tuxedo cat, Frankie, and by the memory of two other unforgettable black and white felines, Boots and Seymour. It is also dedicated to Molly's daughter, aspiring cartoonist Emma Lee Benson.

Thank You's

Ms. Brandenburg would like to thank her many designer friends who helped with the development of this book, including Sheila Schmitz, Marla Nelson, Ron Benson, Ann Gunder, the late Joe Ranft, Lord Carrett, Bob Staake, and ESPECIALLY my designer and layout artist, mind unscrambler, hand holder, and friend, Ron Hasler of Windyhill Design.

Plus the cats. Couldn't have done it without 'em.

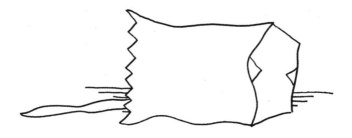

www.everydaycatexcuses.com